Yǔxī, Yìchén
and
Chinese New Year

Written by: Emma Li Illustrated by: Mariya Shevchenko

© Published by Emma Li. All rights reserved.

Yìchén and Yǔxī are siblings. Yìchén is the younger brother, and he is 3 years old. His sister, Yǔxī, is the older one, and she is 7 years old.

The siblings are preparing for the upcoming Chinese New Year. This is a special time for their family, so preparations start much earlier. There are so many things to do!

"Yǔxī, why are we celebrating Chinese New Year?" Yìchén asked.

A long, long time ago, there was a monster named Nian. It has a long head and sharp horns," Yǔxī started her story. "It lived deep in the sea all year round and only shows up every New Year's Eve to eat people and animals. Because of that, on the day of New Year's Eve, people ran far away to mountains to avoid being harmed by the monster.

One day, an old man with white hair and ruddy skin visited the village. He refused to hide in the mountains and decided to scare away the monster. He pasted red papers on doors, burned bamboo to make a loud cracking sound, lighted candles in the houses, and wore red clothes.

When Nian came as usual, he feared the color red and sensed everywhere was fire. Therefore, Nian ran back into water and ever since then, Nian never came back to disturb the villagers. What the man did was successful and when the villagers came back, they were surprised the village had not been destroyed.

After that, every New Year's Eve, people did as the old man instructed and the monster Nian never showed up again. This tradition has been continued until these days and this is the reason we celebrate new year in that way.

"Yǔxī, will the monster never come back for sure?" Yìchén asked.

"Don't be afraid, nothing like that will happen again," Yǔxī said and hugged her brother.

"Kids, we're going shopping!" Mom said. "We have to buy the important things to prepare Christmas dishes.
"Who will be first in the car?" Dad asked. "One, two, three!"

The children hurried to the car and went to the store with their parents.

Yìchén and Yǔxī, together with their parents, choose what to buy. What do you think will be useful for them for the Chinese New Year celebration? Show with your finger what they should buy, and say why?

snacks

watch

toothbrush

rice

red paper for decoration

shovel

helmet

scooter

fish

new clothes

After shopping, Yǔxī entered Yìchén's room.

"Yìchén, what a mess! How many things do you have here? We have to help our parents and clean our house for the upcoming holiday," she said.

"I don't enjoy cleaning," Yìchén replied.

"Cleaning is very important, especially before Chinese New Year!" Yǔxī said. "It helps us get rid of mess, the old things in our lives and make room for new ones. Our house also needs to be prepared for the New Year."

"All right, so be it," Yìchén replied.

Oh, what a mess this is! Help Yìchén and Yǔxī put things in their right place. Point your finger to where they should put the items.

T-shirt

applecore

shoes

color pencils

candy wrapper

paper

pants

T-shirt

wardrobe

wastebasket

desk

The time before the New Lunar Year is the time when we travel to visit our family. This year, grandparents are coming to the Yǔxī and Yìchén family! The next day, kids and parents went to the train station to pick their grandmother and grandfather.

"Grandma!" Yìchén exclaimed cheerfully.
"Hi Grandpa, we missed you," Yǔxī greeted.

"Yìchén, do you know your zodiac sign?" Yǔxī asked.
"No, what is it?" Yìchén replied.
"The signs of the zodiac help to know the nature, strengths, weaknesses and talents of each person. The Chinese zodiac signs are animals and we have 12 of them," Yǔxī explained.
"Mine is a horse. If you don't know what your zodiac sign is, ask our parents or grandparents," said Yǔxī.

Yìchén went to the living room and met his grandmother sitting on the couch.
"Grandma, what is my zodiac sign?" Yìchén asked.
"Each year has its own animal, which is its symbol. Your sign is a dog because you were born in the year of the Dog. According to our horoscope, people like you are brave, loyal and clever.
"And what are the other animals? Tell me about them, Grandma," Yìchén asked.

The first sign of the zodiac is Rat. It's:

smart - it knows a lot, and it's clever

charming - people like how it behaves; pleasant and attractive.

persuasive - it can cause other animals to do or believe something

Rat - shǔ

The second sign of the zodiac is the Ox. It's:

patient - it can wait without complaining or becoming sad

kind - it does and tells people nice things

conservative - it doesn't accept changes. Instead, prefer things to stay as they are.

Ox - niú

The third sign of the zodiac is the Tiger. It's:

authoritative - it has or shows its power and authority

emotional - it feels a lot of emotion

brave - it can do things that scare other people

Tiger - hǔ

The fourth sign of the zodiac is the Rabbit. It's:

popular - many people know and like him

compassionate - it can imagine and feel what other people feel

sincere - it chooses the truth always

Rabbit - tù

The fifth sign of the zodiac is the Dragon. It's:

energetic - it has a lot of energy and moves a lot

fearless - it isn't afraid of different things

charismatic - people like to listen to him and do as it tells

Dragon - lóng

The sixth sign of the zodiac is the Snake. It's:

sociable - it likes to be with people

introvert - it pays more attention to its own thoughts than talk with others

generous - it gives to people a lot. Snake likes to share.

Snake - shé

The seventh sign of the zodiac is the Horse, Yǔxī's zodiac sign. It's:

independent - it likes to do things on its own

impatient - it can't wait a long time for something

enjoy travelling - It loves going a far distance without resting

Horse - mǎ

The next sign is the Goat. Some people refer to the eighth sign as the Sheep. It's:

shy - it doesn't feel brave in front of the others

kind - it's nice to other people

peace-loving - it doesn't like to fight or be nervous in situations

Goat - yán

The ninth sign is the Monkey. It's:

fun - you can have a good time with him with a lot of laugh

energetic - it has a lot of energy. It moves a lot

active - it likes to do a lot of things

Monkey - hóu

The tenth sign is the Rooster. It's:

independent - it likes to do things on its own

practical - it focuses only on important and useful things

hard-working - it works a lot

Rooster - jī

The eleventh sign is the Dog. It's:

patient - it can wait for a long time for something

generous - it gives to people a lot. It likes to share.

faithful - it likes the truth, and it doesn't cheat

Dog - gǒu

The last zodiac is the Pig. It's:

tolerant - it accepts or respects what is different in others

honest - it doesn't lie or cheat on people

luxurious - It likes luxury

"Thank you, Grandma. We have a lot of these signs!" Yìchén said.

Pig - zhū

"Come on Yìchén, time to prepare decorations!" Yǔxī said.
"What are we going to do?" Yìchén asked.
"Grandpa is already preparing Chinese red lanterns. Tomorrow will be Chinese New Year's Eve and together with parents, we will hang couplets, and today we will prepare paper cuts to bring luck and happiness to our home," Yǔxī said.
"What are we going to cut?" Yìchén asked.
"Some animals and plants. Each of them represents a different wish. What do you choose?"

Help Yǔxī and Yìchén choose the paper cuts to make.

The next day was Chinese New Year's Eve. In the morning, the whole family went out in front of the house to hang couplets.

"Why do we hang couplets?" Yìchén asked.
"There is a legend about it," said Dad. "There was a huge peach tree growing on a mountain in the ghost world. To the northeast of the tree, two guards named Shentu and Yulei guarded the entrance to the ghost world. All the evil ghosts were afraid of the two guards because Shentu and Yulei would catch them and then send them to tigers as food.

It was believed that hanging a piece of peach wood with an inscription of the two guards' names on doors could scare evil things away.

Then people started writing two lines with double meanings on the peach wood. Later, red paper replaced the peach wood, which means good luck and happiness. This is the reason we put couplets to welcome the new year, and say best wishes."

In the afternoon, beautiful smells wafted through the house.

"Mmm, what smells so good?" Yǔxī and Yìchén asked.
"We're preparing a New Year dinner," Mom replied.
"The most important dishes are fish, chicken and dumplings. Yǔxī, do you remember the symbolic meanings of each dish we serve during a reunion dinner?" Mom asked.
"Yes… the most important ones are a whole fish and chicken. They mean prosperity and show we are together in our family. Noodles are for happiness and longevity. Spring rolls mean wealth, but my favourite ones are dumplings - the lucky dish!" Yǔxī said. "Are we going to put a lucky coin inside one dumpling?" Yǔxī asked.
"Yes, we will see who has good luck for the New Year!" Mom said. "Do you want to help us?"
"Yes, what can we do?" Yǔxī asked.

Which dish will kids prepare? Help them choose.

Bake Chicken

Make Dumplings

Fill Tangyuan

Stuff Spring Rolls

Wrap in paper Niangao

Cook Fish

Prepare Longevity Noodles

Wash Good Fortune Fruit - tangerines and oranges

It was 5:00 pm in evening and the whole family are gathered in front of the table.
"Kids, before we sit together, let's invite the ghosts of our ancestors to dinner and offer them food," Grandpa said. After giving thanks to their ancestors, the family started their dinner.

"Dad, I see the fish is in front of you. Please enjoy!" Dad said to Grandpa.
"Kids, what is your favourite dish?" Grandma asked.
"Dumplings, of course," Yǔxī said.
"Me, too," Yìchén said. How about you? What is your favourite dish?

"Yìchén, do you want to share one dumpling?" Yǔxī asked.
"Yes, thank you," Yìchén said.

Kids took one dumpling and cut them into two. Then they saw… a coin!

"Mummy, daddy, we are the lucky ones!" Yìchén said.

The whole family applauded.

"Congratulations Yǔxī and Yìchén, you are the luckiest siblings in the world today!" Grandma said.
„…and for the rest of the New Year!" Yǔxī said.

"I think we will make you luckier with our little gift," Grandma said and gave red envelopes to the children.
"Thank you, Grandma, thank you, Grandpa," the kids said.
"But don't open it, now. You should do it later in your room," Mom said.
"Yǔxī, what is inside?" Yìchén asked.
"This is a gift for us; money in the red pocket. We will see later, it's not polite to open it in the presence of the person who give you the gift," Yǔxī said.

All the evening, the family told funny stories and spend a lovely time together. After trying all the dishes, they watched New Year Gala on TV.

"Yìchén, you can't sleep," Yǔxī said. „It's Chinese New Year's Eve, we have to stay up late."
"Why?" Yìchén asked.
"You will see later. I'm sure you will like it a lot," Yǔxī replied.

The clock approached midnight. The New Year bell from the temple next to the family's house rang. The family went outside and saw a spectacular display of fireworks and firecrackers.

"Wow, they're amazing!" Yìchén said.
"I told you, it worths to stay up late on Chinese New Year's Eve," Yǔxī laughed.

These are beautiful fireworks! What are their colors? Let's see.

red - hóng

blue - lán

green - lǜ

yellow - huáng

brown - kāfēi

pink - fěnhóng

orange - chéng

purple - zǐ

The next day was the first day of New Year! The whole family put on new clothes and shared New Year Greetings.

Yǔxī wanted to decorate her hair with glitter on the occasion of the New Year. She went into the room and picked her box of decorations. Suddenly, the box fell from her hands and the glitter spilt onto the floor.

"Mom, can I take a broom to clean up?" she asked.
"Better not Yǔxī, according to New Year's superstition, you should not clean up on New Year's Day, so as not to get rid of happiness in the house," Mom replied. "Put the glitter to the corner, you'll clean it up latter."
"Mom, what else shouldn't we do on New Year's Day?" Yìchén asked.

"You shouldn't clean, wash (including washing your hair) because you can wash away good luck. You shouldn't cry, say negative words, borrow money and void white and black clothes to avoid bad luck. However, you should always focus on things and activities that are related to positive things," Mom said.

Help the kids choose the new clothes to wear for the Chinese New Year. Show with your finger which ones you like best and which are good for Chinese New Year.

During the day, the whole family went to the temple to offer sacrifices. Afterward, they went on the street to see something special.
"Kids, look, the lion dance is about to start!" Dad said and took Yìchén in his arms to let him see better.

Two dancers in red-orange costumes were performing.

"Dad, why are they dancing?" Yìchén asked.
"They are performing the Lion dance to bring prosperity and good luck for the upcoming year," Dad replied.

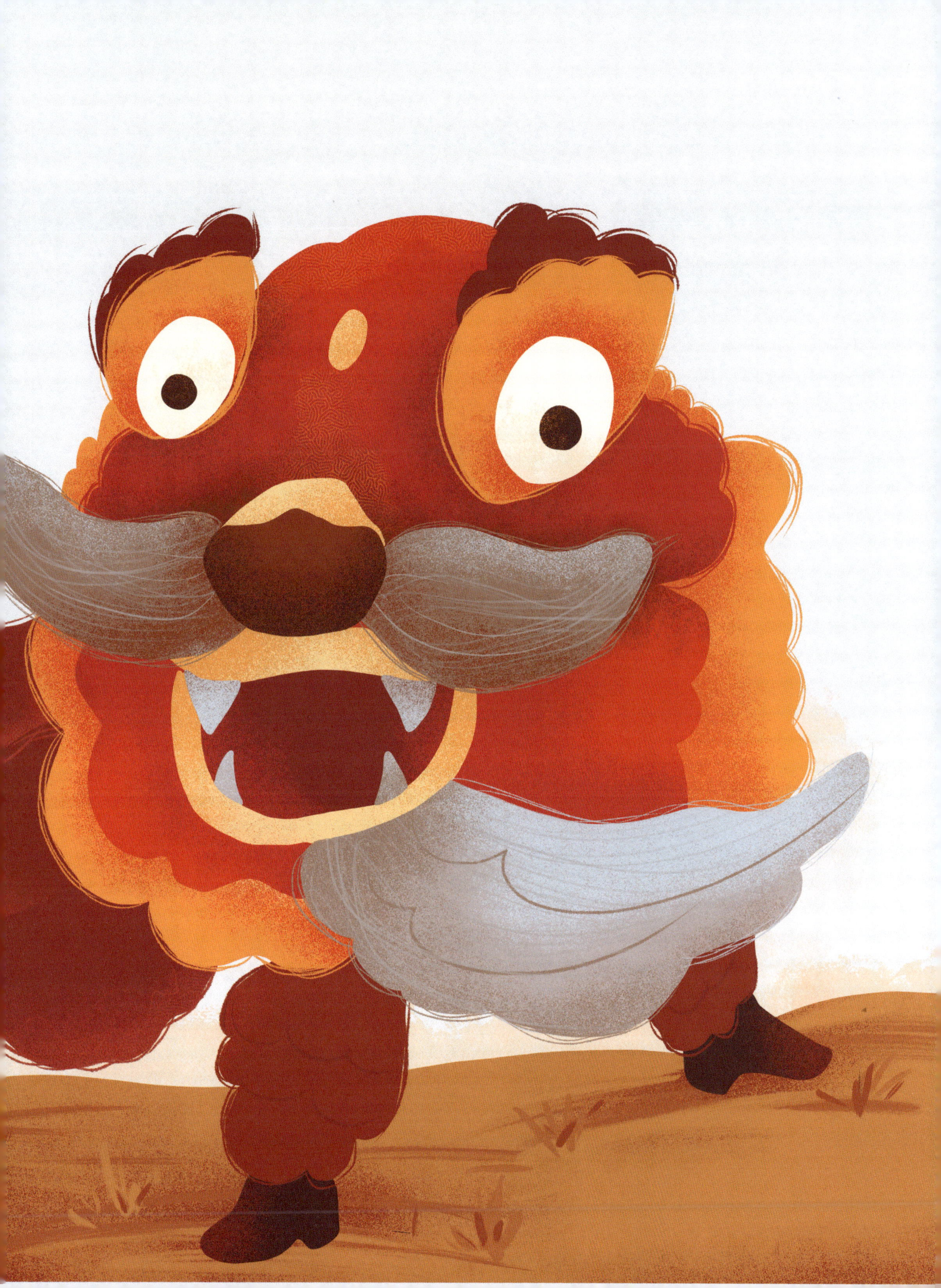

During the Chinese year period, families engage in different things to celebrate new Lunar Year.

They visit their friends and the tombs of their relatives. They offer sacrifices to the God of Wealth, wishing for a luckier and a good year.

After a few days, it's time for the first house-sweep of the New Year.

Eventually, Yǔxī can clean the floor of her room - she's not afraid she would sweep away her good luck for the rest of the year.

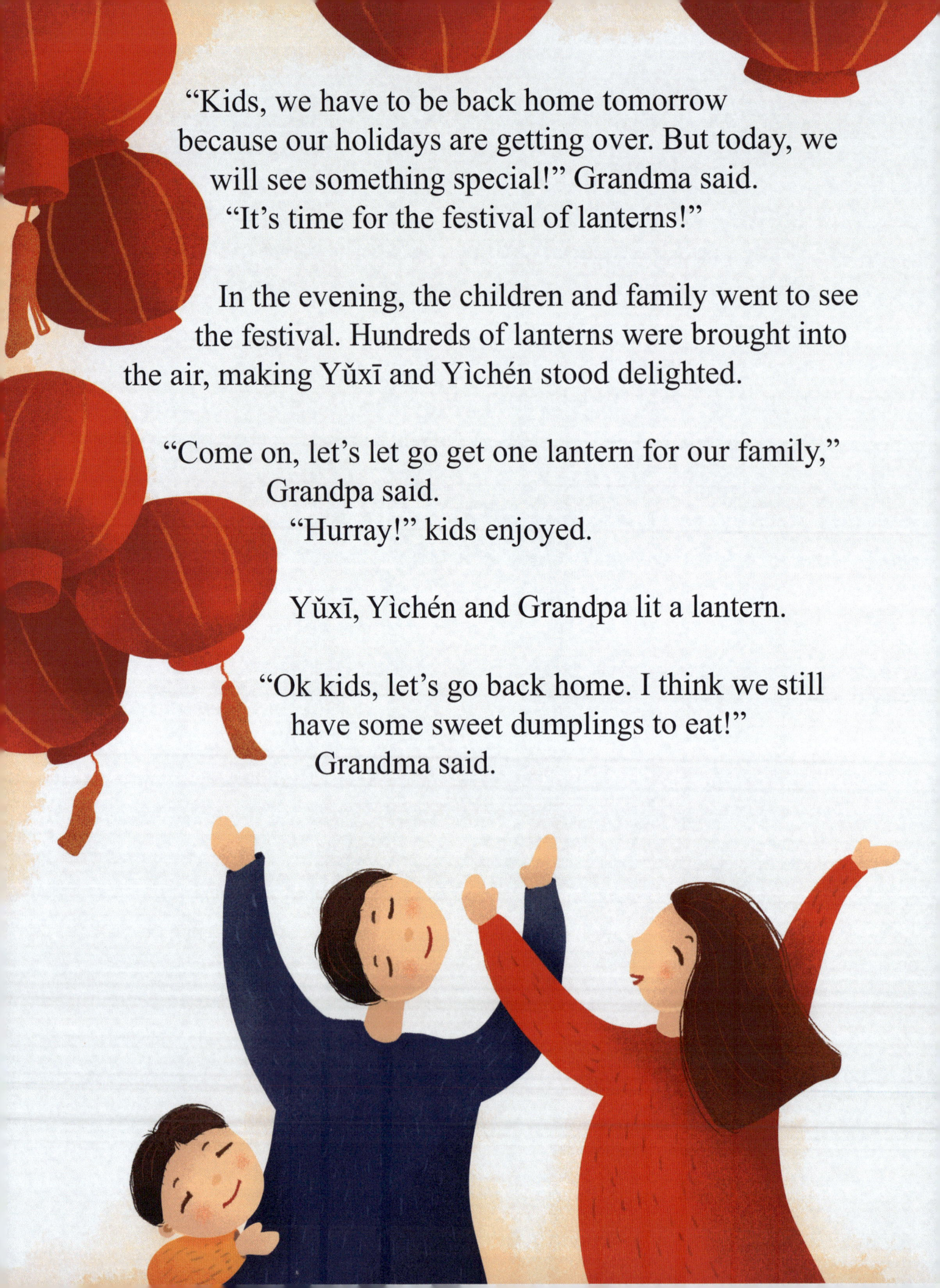

"Kids, we have to be back home tomorrow because our holidays are getting over. But today, we will see something special!" Grandma said.
"It's time for the festival of lanterns!"

In the evening, the children and family went to see the festival. Hundreds of lanterns were brought into the air, making Yǔxī and Yìchén stood delighted.

"Come on, let's let go get one lantern for our family," Grandpa said.
"Hurray!" kids enjoyed.

Yǔxī, Yìchén and Grandpa lit a lantern.

"Ok kids, let's go back home. I think we still have some sweet dumplings to eat!"
Grandma said.

How many lanterns can you see? Let's count!

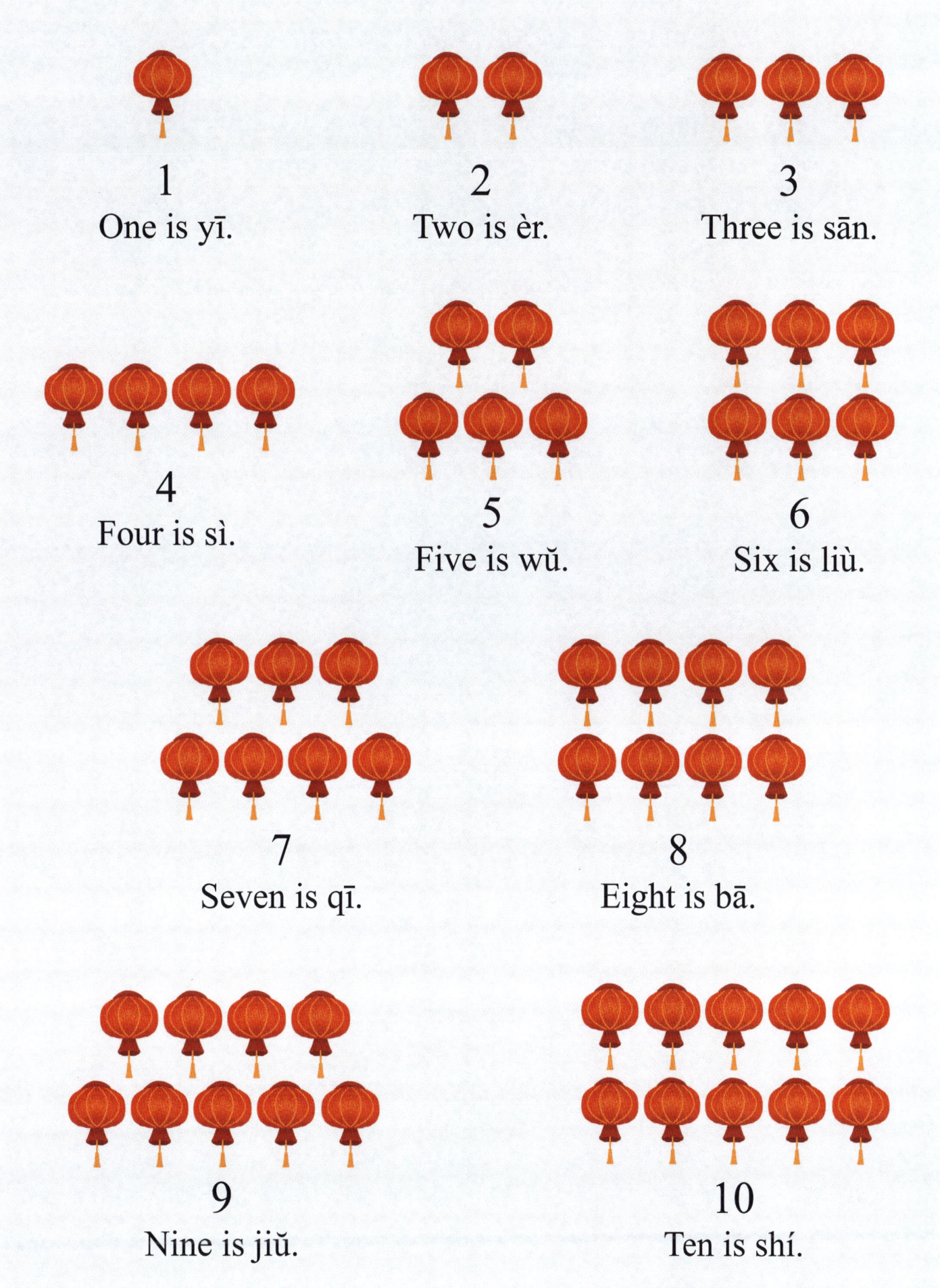

1
One is yī.

2
Two is èr.

3
Three is sān.

4
Four is sì.

5
Five is wǔ.

6
Six is liù.

7
Seven is qī.

8
Eight is bā.

9
Nine is jiǔ.

10
Ten is shí.

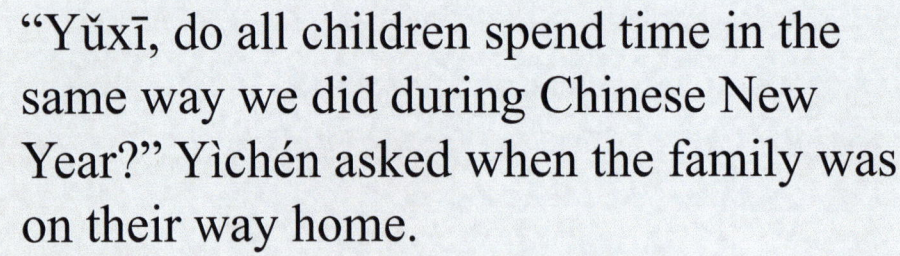

"Yǔxī, do all children spend time in the same way we did during Chinese New Year?" Yìchén asked when the family was on their way home.

"Almost yes, but there are some differences, and that's another story," Yǔxī said.

"I like Chineses New Year," said Yìchén.

"I wonder what New Year will bring to us. Maybe new friends in your kindergarten?" Yǔxī said.

"Let's think about wish."

And you? What is your wish for the Chinese New Year?

HAPPY CHINESE NEW YEAR!

~

XĪNNIÁN KUÀILÈ!

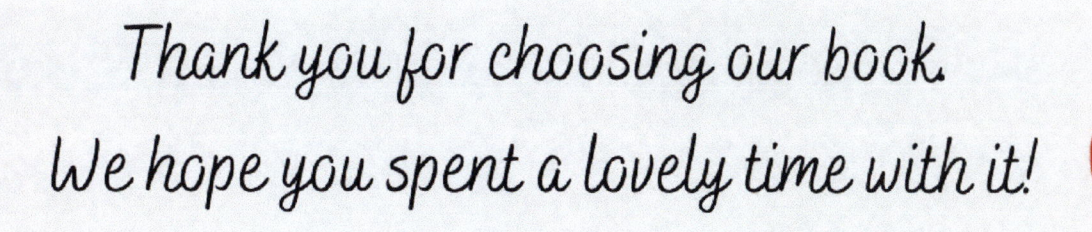

Thank you for choosing our book.
We hope you spent a lovely time with it!

If you like our siblings' story we would appreciate it if you can **share your opinion on Amazon.**

If you want to receive **information about new books from series** or you have any suggestions for our future publications please contact us:

es.publishing.amazon@gmail.com

Printed in Great Britain
by Amazon